To my friend, Eugene,

Dean Rea 2018

Touch All Your Bases

ADVICE FOR MY GREAT-GRANDCHILDREN

Dean Rea

LUMINARE PRESS
WWW.LUMINAREPRESS.COM

Touch All Your Bases: Advice for My Great-Grandchildren

Printed in the United States of America

Luminare Press
467 W 17th Ave
Eugene, OR 97401
www.luminarepress.com

LCCN: 2015959161

ISBN: 978-1-937303-75-4

Acknowledgements

I could not have touched all my bases without the editing help of my wife Lou, the encouragement of my family members and the assistance of my publisher, Patricia Marshall.

Contents

Exploring Choices

Seeking Adventure

Preface

Don't kid yourself. This book of advice was really written for parents as well as for my great-grandchildren. I know, however, that you may not choose to follow all of this advice, but I trust that the journey will be enjoyable as you read through the following chapters.

For the record, I have nine great-grandchildren with the prospect of another half dozen or so showing up during the next decade. I couldn't wait until they all are born to write this book of advice because I don't plan to stick around that long. Granted, I'm in my late 80s and may live for another 20 years or so. You never know about God's plan.

My wife Lou and I reared four children, who begat eight children, who begat the growing audience that I'm addressing in this book. Most members of the clan live in western Oregon. A few scattered elsewhere, but we keep in touch with the help of various electronic gadgets.

While my wife and I are Christians, more liberal than conservative, we realize that many parents follow different belief systems, which really doesn't alter the central message of this book: It's tough being a kid, and it's tough being a parent in any generation. We all need as much help as we can get.

I confess that you will discover a lot of hyperbole in this book because that's how I approach being a great-grandad, and why my great-grandchildren often call me "silly."

"Touch All Your Bases" was advice that my wife and I gave our four athletic children, three of whom played baseball. It also is a reminder that all of us should strive to live a balanced, meaningful life.

GETTING STARTED

QUESTIONING ADVICE

Your word is a lamp to guide my feet and a light for my path.
—Psalms 119:105 NLT

uestion the advice that appears

;randad who's talking, and you things and likes to have fun. ıy of his advice?

that your great-grandad lived on There was no running water nor re he lived. He took a bath every ıb. He didn't watch television or ɔecause TV and computers hadn't ıave mattered because no electrical t rural community.

ked cows every morning and every t know, cows don't take vacations. He also walked behind a team of horses with his hands on plow handles during the spring and helped harvest crops during the fall. He rode to school in a bus like many of you do. One year he walked to and from a one-room school where students in all eight grades met.

Yes, your great-grandad lived in a different world than you do, but he faced many of the same problems and temptations that you face. What he learned during those years proved valuable throughout his life.

For example, he learned that life is an adventure. It may

be frightening and painful at times, but it also can be exciting, enjoyable and rewarding.

That probably explains why your great-grandad often jokes and acts silly. He's determined to find joy in this world rather than wait to find it in the next one. Some folks would say that's bad theology, but it works for your great-grandad and may work for you.

So, when you read my advice about such things as brushing your teeth, negotiating an allowance, playing the piano and watching where you walk, take it with a grain of salt.

Remember, however, that your parents want the best for you even though you may feel that they sometimes set the boundaries a bit narrow and call too many "time outs."

In the chapters that follow, I encourage you to think outside of what I call "the box." Not so far that you fall off the earth and go into orbit in space, but you get the picture.

You and I know that your parents probably will read the advice that follows and will know how to help you grow into the person that God—and they—want you to be. Keep in mind, however, that you have a responsibility in helping chart your future.

So, if any of the advice that I or anyone else offers fails to measure up, take seriously the words from the Bible that introduce each chapter. You can't go wrong following the advice of your heavenly father.

Honoring Your Parents

Honor your father and your mother so that you may live long in the land the Lord your God is giving you.

—Exodus 20:5 NIV

As you probably know, this commandment shows up in the Old Testament of the Bible. Even though it's as old as the hills, this command is still worth thinking about, especially when you're a kid.

First of all, we need to figure out what the word, honor, means. In your case, it probably means that you do what your parents ask you to do, and you do what you are expected to do as a member of a family.

Of course, it also means that way down deep in your heart you really like your parents. You know that when the chips are down, your dad will come to your defense when someone threatens you and that your mother will bake you peanut butter cookies even though you did something wrong.

When I think of honor, I think of being a private during what is called basic training in the Army. When the sergeant gives you an order, you stand at attention and answer one of three ways: Yes sir, no sir or no excuse. You don't whine, you don't argue, you don't cry, you don't pout. You do what you're told to do.

Let me explain how it works in many families.

If you're lucky, you have your own room in your house. That may be your room, but your folks still are in charge. Like the sergeant in the Army, your mother and father want you to learn how to take care of things in your room. So, you're expected to make your bed each day, to keep your clothes off the floor and to sweep the place out every week or so.

My folks made me learn how to play the piano. I wasn't good at it, but I learned how to read music and later to enjoy listening to all kinds of music. You wouldn't believe it, but I still play the piano today. I also grew to love listening to all kinds of music.

While I was growing up, I often thought my mom and dad didn't appreciate me enough, didn't let me do things I wanted to do, played favorites and treated my brother better than me.

Later, I learned that they were teaching me how to live, love and lead in this world, a task that is never easy for a kid or for a parent.

And don't go bellyaching if your father isn't your real dad or that your mother isn't your real mom or that your mom and dad aren't your real parents. Down deep in their hearts, they love you and want the best for you. The same goes if you only have one parent. That person needs your support and love for a family to succeed in today's world.

So, what's the prize if we honor our moms and dads? The Lord says we'll be rewarded. That may not happen while you're growing up, but it will happen more often than you suspect. And rewards often appear in the most unexpected places.

I have been rewarded because of the good memories I have of my mom and dad—and even of my brother. I hope that you will feel that way, too, about your mom and dad. They are special people who love you and want the best for you even through they may nag you to brush your teeth and to clean up your room.

Remember, your answer should be yes sir, no sir or no excuse.

Negotiating an Allowance

And my God will meet all your needs according to His glorious riches in Christ Jesus.

—Philippians 4:19 NIV

Hopefully, you receive an allowance from your parents. Make certain they don't insist that you save all of it for college or tie the allowance to taking out the trash, washing dishes or keeping your room clean. That's not an allowance. It's blackmail.

So, here's a plan, actually several plans:

First, negotiate a weekly allowance. By negotiate, I mean "put the squeeze on mom and dad for a good deal." Your parents may offer a monthly allowance. Won't work because if you are like me, you'll lose interest in money if it only appears every 30 days or so.

Second, you need to hold out for BIG money. We're talking dollars, not pennies.

How about a dollar that matches each year of your age? That means that when you are 10, you receive $10. Now, we're talking REAL money. (If inflation sets in, go for broke.)

You also are talking BIG responsibility. So, how do you spend the stuff? Here's something to consider.

First, create a budget like your parents do—or should. Permit them to make suggestions, but it's your budget. So, make your own decision. If you want to spend it all on candy, make certain that your parents have good dental insurance.

Second, don't allow anyone to talk you into saving all of your allowance for college. Might as well not have an allowance or a budget if you're forced into this decision. Granted, you can save some of the money for a rainy day, but how about creating a grown-up budget?

Example: Split your budget into thirds: (1) to spend, (2) to give and (3) to save. That way you know how much you have to spend on something you want. Example: candy bars. You know how much you have to give to your Sunday School or to some worthy cause and how much to save.

Better yet, if a member of the family or friend knows how to invest money, ask them for help in putting a few dollars in the market or some method of earning more than routine interest. If you start saving now, you may have enough money to retire when you're 95 years old.

However, if you have your eye on a big-ticket item like a bicycle, then save money for a few weeks or months and purchase it rather than wait for Santa Claus to come to your rescue.

Keep in mind that your parents are smart enough to know that granting an allowance and permitting you to decide how to spend it will teach important life lessons.

Best wishes as you negotiate the terms of your contract. If you end up without an allowance or lose it because you failed to take out the trash, get in touch with great-grandad. I'll drop by your house and slip you a candy bar.

Getting a Pet

The wolf will live with the lamb, the leopard will lie down with the goat, the calf and the lion and the yearling together; and a little child will lead them.

—Isaiah 11:6 NIV

Most kids want a pet. Some are luckier than others when it comes to getting a kitten, a puppy or some other critter to call your pal.

I wanted an elephant, but mom said she wouldn't let me bring it in the house at night. So, I got a cat. His name was Tom, and he usually showed up at the barn at milking time. I wasn't allowed to bring a pet in the house. Actually, it didn't matter because Tom was wild, and I could never catch him or pet him.

Pets are cute when they are born. Who doesn't like to hold a kitten or a puppy even though they wiggle and sometimes lick you in the face. You look forward to playing with your pet when you get home from school, and sometimes you get to take your pet to bed with you at night.

Then after awhile, you find something that is more fun than playing with your pet. Maybe its playing baseball or soccer. Maybe tennis or computer games. Normally, you can't take a cat or a dog to watch you play these games. So, you leave your pet at home.

When you return home, you're tired and hungry. Before you can rest or eat your meal, your mom reminds you to take care of your pet. Take it outdoors for a walk. Clean the litter box. At that point you will discover that your pet isn't so cute anymore.

Of course, you need to repeat taking care of your pet in the morning and hope that mom will fill in for you while you're at school. Then a pet can become a problem if the family takes a vacation, and you can't take your pet with you. So, you leave it with a neighbor or take it to a kennel.

So, here is my advice if you're thinking about getting a pet.

First, make sure that you can take care of your pet 24 hours a day every day of the year for as long as the pet lives. (A friend of mine once had a dog that lived 26 years.)

Second, save a big chunk of your allowance to buy pet food and to pay the veterinarian when your pet gets sick or hurt.

Third, either take the pet with you or make arrangements for someone to take care of your pet when your family is away from home. (Neighbors get upset when they hear a dog outside the house barking all day long.)

Better yet, get an elephant for a pet. You can have fun riding an elephant around town. The elephant can use its trunk to play catch with you and to give you a shower at night. Of course, an elephant would eat a lot, and you might have trouble getting an elephant in the house.

So, take my advice and don't get a pet until you're about 55 years old. Then rather than settle on a kitten, a puppy, a bird, a snake, an alligator or a dog.

Get an elephant.

Minding Your Manners

Be devoted to one another in love. Honor one another above yourselves.

—Romans 12:10 NIV

I think of a kitten when I think of manners. You know about kittens. They're usually cute, cuddly, playful, friendly. You want to make sure they are comfortable, well fed and in a safe place.

That's one way to think about manners, which means you're on your best behavior and that you want to please another person. It's easy, of course, to treat a friend nicely. It's not so easy to treat someone nicely who's been punching you in the nose or stealing your stuff.

But we should treat everyone with love and respect like you would treat a kitten even though you would rather kick someone in the shins.

Keep in mind, too, that we are expected to follow customs or special practices passed along from generation to generation.

Here's an example:

It may be hard to believe but your parents are my grandchildren. When my grandsons became teenagers, I told them they should open the car door for their girlfriends when they get in and out of a car. I told my grandaughters never go on a second date with a guy who fails to mind his manners and to open the door of the car for them.

Of course, most guys forget to open the car doors for the girls after they're married.

I have another example:

When one of my grandsons was just a little fellow, he and his sisters visited his grandmother and me. Dinner was served buffet style. As you know, buffet means that you take a plate and walk down a line, picking out the stuff you want to eat. It means you can skip the broccoli and load up on mashed potatoes and gravy.

Our grandson was first in line because he was the youngest member of the clan. He filled his plate, rushed to the table and began to eat. Meanwhile, one of his sisters panicked, knowing that you don't begin eating at grandad's house until someone says a prayer of blessing.

"Wait," my grandaughter yelled at her brother. "We haven't said the pledge, yet."

Saying a prayer before you eat is a lot like saying the Pledge of Allegiance before a public meeting or during a military ceremony. We're minding our manners, being respectful.

Minding your manners also means that you look for ways to help someone. Maybe it's a simple as helping your mom set the table, washing the dishes or cleaning the litter box of that kitten you love so much.

When you help someone, keep in mind that person may not want to be helped. You know the story about the Boy Scout who insisted on helping an elderly person across the street. Turns out the person didn't want to cross the street.

If all of this doesn't make much sense to you, follow a simple rule: Do unto others as you would have them do unto you. That rule applies to people as well as to kittens.

Washing Your Hands

The fear of the Lord is pure, enduring forever.

—Psalms 19:9 NIV

Your parents know that I have a rule: Thou shalt wash your hands before you eat. It sounds scriptural although it really deals with keeping bad bugs out of your body. No one wants to be sick and throw up. So, pay attention to what I say.

First, I want to tell a story about your mother. When she was a girl, she joined five of her cousins, their great-grandma Lou and me for a trip to the Oregon Coast. We stayed in a three-bedroom suite, swam in the hotel's pool, walked on the beach, played games and ate our meals there and at various restaurants.

When we arrived at the hotel, a few of the girls wanted to know what rules they were expected to follow.

"Thou shalt wash your hands before you eat," was my reply.

"But, grandad, aren't their any more rules?"

"No," I answered.

"When do we have to go to bed?"

"When you want to."

"But we have to go to bed by 9 o'clock at home."

"You're not at home."

With shrieks of delight, the first-day adventure took off and continued non-stop late into the night. As your mother may recall, at the conclusion of the second night most of the girls were exhausted and flopped into bed long before 9 o'clock.

Now, why would I want you to wash your hands before eating?

When I was a boy, I lived on a farm and helped milk cows each morning and evening. We sold the milk from six Jersey cows to a creamery. That milk later showed up in jugs and bottles in stores. People purchased and drank the milk, and it had to be clean.

So, I was required not only to wash my hands but also to wash the undercarriage of the cow before I sat down and began milking. And the pail had to be clean, too.

My parents also taught that what I put in my mouth as well as in my heart should be clean. But washing your hands wasn't so simple because we had to pump our water from a well and bring it into the house where it was heated on a wood stove.

When I was a boy, I washed my hands by splashing water and rubbing my hands together a couple of times. Later, I learned a better way to wash the bugs off my hands. Put a bit of soap on your wet hands. Rub your hands together and fingers inside fingers. Then do the same thing with one hand over the back of the other hand. Then switch sides.

I suppose that keeping your hands and heart clean are a lot alike. You have to work at it a bit. However, don't let anyone fool you by suggesting that "cleanliness is next to Godliness." That rule ain't in the Bible. My rule about washing your hands ain't in the Bible either, but you had better follow it if you want to eat at my table.

Drinking Your Milk

Like newborn infants, long for the pure spiritual milk (so) you may grow up into salvation…

—1 Peter 2:2 ESV

"Drink your milk," was a command that I heard often at the breakfast table while I lived on a farm. "It will make you grow strong," mom would say.

Those words fell on deaf ears because I figured I already was growing as fast as the weeds that I had to pull up in the garden. Anyway, I didn't like to drink milk unless it was cooled in the cellar. Milk is warm when it comes out of a cow, and I didn't like warm milk.

On the other hand, cats like warm milk. They would show up in the barn while I was milking and would sit a few feet away with big smiles on their faces.

I would squirt milk into their mouths. A lot of the milk ended up on their faces, but they had no problem rubbing paws across their faces and licking the extra milk from their paws.

I often wondered how cows manufactured milk. I knew they spent all day eating grass and chewing what is called a "cud," which is grass they burp up and re-chew when they're taking a "coffee break."

Later, I learned a cow's stomach is like a store with four departments. One sells shoes, the other sells underwear, etc. Actually, the largest department can hold up to 50 gallons of partially digested food. It's too difficult for me to understand and to explain how all of the departments work. All I know is that cows manufacture milk, which I had to squeeze out of them every morning and every night.

Today, I understand that machines milk cows. Now, that's good news, but I wonder what barnyard cats think about that?

As a little kid, you probably hear people tell you that milk is good for your teeth. That may be true, but I wondered why my first set of teeth fell out of my mouth after I was forced to drink milk with my meals?

The tooth fairy probably was to blame. At least I got paid for losing my first set of teeth. I would leave what they called a baby tooth under my pillow at night, and it would be gone the next morning. Folks said the tooth fairy took the tooth. Fortunately, the fairy always left a penny under my pillow.

Eventually, I grew a second set of teeth. Then I discovered that it cost a lot more than a penny to lose a tooth, and the tooth fairy didn't help pay for it.

I still have most of my teeth, and I still don't drink milk. I must confess, however, that I pour milk on my cereal and that I use milk when I bake a batch of biscuits.

In the event you are forced to drink the stuff, mix it with chocolate—lots of chocolate.

Your great-grandad has spent a lot of time around milk. He may prefer to drink coffee, but you can't go wrong by using milk to make home-made ice cream, which I write about in the next chapter.

Churning Ice Cream

So, whether you eat or drink, or whatever you do, do all to the glory of God.

—1 Corinthians 10:31 ESV

Most kids like ice cream. Some like vanilla. Some like orange. Some like tutti frutti. Most everyone likes chocolate.

Vanilla, however, tops my list. I've been eating vanilla ice cream since before I could walk. Maybe before I was born. Anyway, my parents, their parents and their grandparents ate ice cream—and they made ice cream.

Yummy stuff. Only you have to mix eggs and a bunch of other stuff, including vanilla, and crank it in a tub until the mixture turns to ice cream. It's called home-made ice cream, and you have to crank it by hand or it isn't really home-made.

Don't let anyone put anything but vanilla in the tub. If someone likes peach, strawberry, chocolate or turnip ice cream, tell then to add the topping after the vanilla ice cream is dipped into dishes.

This may sound like a lot of work, and it is. You must put a lot of thought and sweat into something like this if you expect it to be successful. It's like riding a bicycle. You need to peddle the critter and sweat some if you expect to arrive at your destination.

Making ice cream is a lot like that, especially turning the crank until the milk and other stuff freezes. A paddle in the ice cream tank helps freeze the mixture. You want to be first in line to lick the ice cream from the paddle after it is taken from the can. Yummy stuff, but watch out because the ice cream can run down your chin onto your birthday suit. And if you eat home-made ice cream too fast, it will give you an instant headache.

I'll let you in on a little secret if you promise not to tell anyone. It may take 15 or 20 minutes to crank the freezer handle until the ice cream freezes. Make sure that you are first in line to crank the freezer handle and leave the hard cranking to your dad or to a big brother or sister.

This cranking session has become a tradition in our family. Big and little folks gather around the freezer and talk while they crank. We make home-made ice cream during family gatherings, even when it rains or snows.

In case your mom doesn't have a recipe, I'll share mine, which was handed down for generations. You'll need a six-quart ice cream maker.

4 quarts 2 percent milk

6 to 8 eggs

4 ½ cups sugar

¼ teaspoon salt

4 tablespoons pure vanilla

Bring sugar and two quarts of the milk to scalding. Stir so the sugar won't scorch or stick to the bottom of the pan. Pour the scalded milk mixture over slightly beaten eggs while stirring as your pour. Cool. Pour mixture into canister. Add vanilla and enough 2 percent milk to nearly fill the canister.

Start churning.

Talking to Your Teeth

There will be weeping and gnashing of teeth...

—Luke 13:28 ESV

You probably will live to be a hundred years old. So, listen closely. I'm talking to your teeth.

You may have read stories about George Washington. He's considered to be the father of our country. Unfortunately, he had bad teeth. Wore false ones made of wood.

You also may have seen movies, TV shows and pictures of pioneers as they traveled west. Remember how pearly white and perfect their teeth looked? Well, most of the real pioneers probably didn't smile a whole lot in those days because their teeth were either missing or rotted. Dentists in those days didn't clean teeth like your dental hygienist, paint teeth with fluoride or drill out the bad stuff. Dentists pulled teeth with pliers.

A few folks, however, were lucky. For example, my grandmother had perfect teeth until the day she died in her 70s. No missing teeth and no cavities. She was a farm girl who married a farmer. She sweetened stuff with honey, fruit and berries grown on a farm. Brushed her teeth after every meal with a rag. Tooth brushes were invented after she died.

Unfortunately, my father was a city boy who probably dumped sugar on his cereal and drank a lot of soda pop. By the time he was in his 30s, he had all of his teeth pulled and began wearing false ones. He never liked them because he said that stuff got stuck between his upper plate and the roof of his mouth. Now, we won't discuss what the "stuff" was, but you get the idea.

While I was a newspaper reporter, I interviewed a dentist who was retiring after practicing his profession for nearly 50 years. I asked him a lot of questions. He said many of his patients paid their bills with chickens, eggs, hogs and other stuff rather than with money. Seems a lot of his patients were poor farm folks.

The dentist said they didn't fix teeth in those days. They pulled them. Then I asked him how many teeth he had pulled during his career.

He replied, "About a wagon load."

During my day, dentists drilled the bad stuff out of a tooth and filled the cavity with silver. Later, they filled teeth with white stuff, especially front teeth. Then they started putting caps on teeth, and as you know, dentists can now replace teeth. It's a piece of cake. They hammer a peg in your jaw bone, put a fake tooth on the peg and you're good as new. All it costs is more than you will get as an allowance for about 40 years.

So, my advice is to brush your teeth after every meal. If you don't have a toothbrush, give me a call. I'll loan you mine. Don't forget to floss. That's when you run a stringy thing up and down between your teeth. Be careful, however, and don't wreck your gums while flossing. Visit your dentist regularly and don't drink too many Slurpees.

In case you don't know, a Slurpee is a soft drink that is filled with a lot of sugar and stuff that may not be friendly to your teeth. But I love to drink Slurpees. I also brush my teeth.

KEEPING A JOURNAL

"Altogether, Methuselah lived a total of 969 years..."

—Genesis 5:27 NIV

People lived a long time during Bible times. Today, you should expect to live until you're at least a hundred. Meanwhile, I have a word of advice: Keep a journal of important events in your life and in the life of your family.

My grandmother traveled west across the country in a covered wagon to Kansas when she was a girl. She told me that her job was to pick up dry cow chips to fuel the campfire each evening. Unfortunately, I don't know much else about her childhood, and she didn't leave any written history.

The same happened with my parents. I know my father served in the Navy during World War I and met my mother after she graduated from the University of Kansas. It would have been interesting to know something about their courtship, but I never asked and they never mentioned it.

Your great-grandma Lou did a better job of keeping track of family history. She kept a journal in which she recorded our first date on December 4, 1948. It was a spur-of-the-moment date after a football game. Your great-grandma writes:

"When trying to find a parking spot near the theater, a police officer pulled us over to the side of the street and said Dean had run a red light. Oh, no! I was so worried. I thought I was going to have to go to jail, and I'd have to call my parents for money to bail me out. However, the officer received an emergency call and had to leave but gave Dean a verbal warning about running red lights.

"The movie was supposed to be a scary one, but it wasn't and all during the show Dean would ask, 'Are you scared, yet?' I wondered if I said 'yes' he would try to put his arm around me."

Much of our early family history resides in your great-grandma's book, which she titled, "Moving in the Fast Lane." It records the 25 moves we made during our first 53 years of marriage.

Fortunately, several of my grandchildren are keeping track of personal and family history. It's called journaling. I urge you to keep a journal, too. Here are some guidelines:

First, make it a practice to write down important events in your life. Don't wait. At the top of the page, write the day, month and year.

Second, include all types of information, including what happened, what was said and how you feel about an event.

Third, don't let anyone read your journal. It's private because you may write stuff you don't want anyone else to know. If a parent insists on reading your journal, hide it under your bed or behind a toilet bowl.

Fourth, don't lose your journals. Some day they may be important.

For example, I can't remember the year that I learned to ride a bicycle or when my lower front tooth was chipped during a boxing match. I wondered the other night how much my parents paid for Patsy, a garden horse that was blind in one eye. She must have been at least as old as Methuselah. Unfortunately, I didn't keep a journal.

Writing to Grandma

Then those who feared the Lord spoke with each other, and the Lord listened to what they said.

—Malachi 3:16 NLT

Dear Grandma:

How are you? I am just fine.

Johnnie

How many letters have you read that are written this way? Maybe a hundred. Some are written on paper. Others are written on electronic devices. It doesn't matter how the letter is written. What matters is what you tell grandma about what's happening in your life.

If you are like I was when I was a kid nearly a hundred years ago, grandma was happy to learn that I was still alive enough to write her a meaningless note. However, grandma really wanted to learn more about what was going on in my life.

As you may know, today I teach kids how to write. One of our assignments is to write a letter to grandma. It must be at least 200 words long, and it needs to be signed.

So, let's work together and write a letter to grandma. Grab a pencil and a piece of paper, and let's begin.

On the top line write the month, day and year. Then write:

Dear Grandma,

Its been raining hear the last 2 days. The watter in the kreek out back is running over the bankes and washed the dog hous down the driveway into the streat. We got it out of the streat before any kars ran into it.

I ran into a kar with my bike last weak. Didn't hurt the bike, but it dented dad's front door.

I'm doing OK in skool, but I don't like all the home work. We have to do math and I can't do math. I'd rather play basketbal. Dad put a hoop on the garaje but its so high I can't make baskets.

My sister has a boy friend. He's kinda goofy. He's not old enof to drive a kar. So, my mom has to drive them to the movies.

Thanks for the birthday gift. I'll read the book as soon as I get time. Rite now I'm busy playing a kool video game. You ud like it. I'll teach it 2 you when you come down for Crismus.

Love,

Johnnie

WOW, you've written the letter. Before you send it to grandma, a couple of words of advice:

- Don't let anyone read or correct your letter.
- If you send it by mail, make certain that the address is correct and that you put a stamp on the envelope.
- Don't worry about the spelling. Just stuff the letter in an envelope and mail the critter before Christmas.

Shifting Gears

Playing Games

How many books are there in the Bible?

—A question in a game that great-grandad played as a child.

Now, put away your electronic gadgets and join me in a real game.

First, we'll play chess so that you can develop your brain.

Then we'll play board games where you'll have to match wits with a real person. Meanwhile, we can talk about what's happening in your world while we move checkers or marbles across a board or build a jigsaw puzzle.

Or go outdoors and play hide-and-seek. It's a game where one person closes his/her eyes while other kids scatter and hide. Or you can bob for apples, climb a tree or roll down a hill in an old tire.

In my day, farm families got together on Saturday nights for a potluck dinner, games and visiting. Yes, the grown-ups played games, too, but that's getting ahead of my story.

We kids often played what we called fox-and-geese on nights when the moon was shining. We would divide into two groups. One group would be the geese and scatter around a 40-acre farm. The other group would be the foxes, who would try to find the geese. The foxes had lanterns to light their way. The geese depended on the moon to find hiding spots.

One night I was a goose and became separated from the other geese. I hid behind a bush on the other side of the 40 acres and waited for the foxes to appear. As I waited, I worried that the goblins might get me.

I sat behind that bush for a loooooooong time and wondered what happened to the foxes. Eventually, I decided to give up and went in search of the foxes only to discover that they had tired of the game and were now playing carroms.

That's another game you should learn to play. It develops hand-and-eye coordination and places you under real stress as you play a game your folks probably never heard of.

There are advantages playing my kind of games:

- First, you competed with real people.
- Second, the games I played don't cost anything. Most were handed down from generation to generation.
- Third, you often got to move around rather than wear out the seat of your pants while sitting in front of an electronic device.
- Fourth, you can lose valuable stuff if you play some of my games. Marbles, for instance. In that game you round up a dozen or so of your marbles and call one a shooter. You and your opponent place a few marbles in a circle drawn in the dirt and take turns shooting. You get to keep all of the marbles that you hit and drive outside the circle. In my case, I wasn't a good shooter. So, I usually lost all of my marbles. That game teaches you not to play marbles for "keeps" if you're a poor shooter.
- Finally, if you play my games, you may learn that losing can be REAL painful. I remember that my friends and I once played a game on Halloween and tipped over a couple of outhouses. I got a whipping later, which parents don't do anymore. Which proves that you've got it easy being a great-grandkid today.

Enjoying Your Wheels

Their arrows are sharp, all their bows are strung; their horses' hoofs seem like flint, their chariot wheels like a whirlwind.

—Isaiah 5:28 NIV

I loved to ride a bike when I was a boy. I especially liked to ride it fast like a whirlwind. In those days we didn't wear helmets. If we crashed, we hurt anything that hit the ground. I never crashed. Not once. I was lucky.

Riding a bike is a lot like growing up. You start with a little bike, one with training wheels. Those extra wheels on each side of the bike keep you from wobbling all over the yard and crashing.

Then, you grow big enough to get a "real" bike, maybe one that Santa Claus leaves beside the Christmas tree. You know that mom and dad really are Santa Claus, but you don't want to spoil a good thing. So, you continue to "believe" in Santa Claus until you are about 23 years old. Then you're ready for a car.

Meanwhile, you must prove that you're grown up and can ride a bike all by yourself. When I was a boy, bicycle tires were big things. Now they are thin, tiny things, which make it possible to really speed down a hill.

But mom and dad will insist that they help you keep the bike upright while you learn to ride without training wheels. So, strap on a helmet and get on the bike. It's easier to ride a girl's bike because it doesn't have a high bar between the frame and the seat.

In any event, your folks will find a level place for you to

take your first ride. Usually the place will be covered with grass, which may mess up your pants if you fall but won't break any bones.

I remember that my dad took me out on the dirt road in front of our farm house and helped me on my first ride. He held on for awhile, then turned me loose. I pedaled the bike a time or two, and my dad cheered me on. Only I started to wobble, and he grabbed me and kept me from falling.

My dad continued to keep me from falling for a long time. Then I got the hang of riding, and he turned me loose. I was so happy as I pedaled that bike that I forgot about the hill. The bike picked up speed at the top, and I screamed for help, certain that I would crash and die. Only I didn't crash, and I grew to love riding a bicycle.

Later, I learned to drive a car when I was 12, which was easier because it had four wheels. My folks often didn't have time to drive to town for supplies needed on the farm, especially during harvest time. So, I did the driving. Unfortunately, today you will have to wait forever before you can get a driver's license. To make matters worse, you have to pass a test.

In any event, wheels are important in our lives. Make sure, however, that you check out where the journey may take you. Of course, you won't always arrive at the place you had in mind. That's okay because life is an adventure. You may fall off a bike and suffer bruises, but the journey also can be exciting and lots of fun.

For those of you who read the Bible, remember Ephesians 6:1, which suggests that if you put on your spiritual helmet, elbow and knee pads, there's no reason to fear where your wheels may take you.

Fighting Comes Natural

But if you bite and devour one another, watch out that you are not consumed by one another.

—Galatians 5:15 ESV

Let me tell you a story about fighting. It started years and years ago in Scotland where our family originated.

Some of our ancestors were members of the Macrae Clan, which did a lot of fighting. It may not be true, but the story passed down from olden times tells how some of our ancestors survived because they ran.

That's right. They ran from the fight, and that's what many of our clan members have been doing ever since.

That doesn't mean that we won't stand up for what's right. It means that we know when to run and when to fight.

If you're a little kid and you have a sister or a brother, you're going to fight one another.

Doesn't matter what your parents tell you about sharing your toys, not picking on one another, being kind to one another.

Fighting is part of growing up.

I know because my brother and I yelled at one another, pushed one another and "told on one another" when we were kids. We cried and pouted when we thought we got the short end of the stick and when one of us got the wishbone of the fried chicken and the other one didn't.

Brothers and sisters fight one another for a number of

reasons. Your folks won't tell you, but fighting keeps brothers and sisters from loving one another physically. (If you don't understand what I'm saying, you can turn to the chapter about the birds and bees.)

As you grow up, you will learn how to settle differences without slugging someone with a fist.

And you will learn that you don't have to run from a fight.

First, take a time-out, which means you step outside yourself and figure out whether you can settle the problem without slugging someone.

Second, you soon will realize that your pride has been hurt and that you can settle the problem with a handshake.

Third, if the other person is bigger than you and won't try to settle the problem without a fistfight, then run.

As you grow up and leave home, you will discover all kinds of things you want to fight. I'm not talking about people. I'm talking about what is called injustice, hatred, jealousy and a lot of things over which you may have no control.

You can, however, be a person who seeks to make peace before you fight, someone who sees the good rather than the evil in people and someone who is willing to work out your differences with another person.

I met a guy like that and decided to follow him. He didn't run from a fight. He just knew how to deal with enemies without raising his voice or his fists. He tells me how I can fight what is called the good fight without punching someone in the jaw. I pray that you learn this lesson, too.

ACQUIRING KNOWLEDGE, WISDOM

An intelligent heart acquires knowledge, and the ear of the wise seeks knowledge.

—Proverbs 18:15 ESV

So, how do you get knowledge? And how does getting knowledge make you wise?

Well, people think your great-grandad is wise because he's old. REAL old. Age, however, doesn't have anything to do with knowledge nor with being wise. You can be knowledgeable and wise in a lot of things even when you're little.

First, you acquire, or get, knowledge by learning to read and then reading something other than comic books and playing computer games. Second, you begin collecting information, going to school and finding out what life is about.

Work at it hard enough, and you will collect a lot of knowledge. Work at what you learn long enough, and you might become wise.

For example, I collected a lot of information while working on a farm when I was a boy. I learned how to place harness on horses, to hitch them to a plow and to guide them with leather reins while the plow cut a furrow in the soil. That's called knowledge.

If I had continued to live and to work on a farm, I would have collected a lot of information and experience during the past 80 years. My neighbors might consider me a wise farmer because of my knowledge and experience working with animals and equipment.

It helps, too, if you begin learning something about reading, writing and arithmetic when you enter school. In other words, you can acquire knowledge by getting an education.

I thought that I would never get out of school. I spent years and years in grade school, in junior high, in high school and in college. Would you believe that I sat in classrooms for more than 14 years of my life. When I finally graduated from college, I joined the Air Force and was sent to school AGAIN.

Well, at that point, I had acquired a lot of information, but I didn't have much of a chance to see if it worked. So, I began using the knowledge that I had picked up in school. I enjoyed some success as well as failure as I began rearing a family and working as a journalist.

Eventually, I acquired so much information and so much experience and grew so old that people started thinking I was wise. Maybe I'm wise. Maybe I'm not. In any event, I decided to offer some advice to you, my great-grandchildren. Some of the things I've learned may be of help to you. Here are some of the important ones about information and knowledge:

Investigate both sides of a coin. This applies to all kinds of issues, including religious, social, political. If you are unaware of "the other side" of an issue, you will be neither knowledgeable nor wise.

Walk in another person's shoes. In other words, don't judge another person until you know that person's story. Better yet, don't judge.

Learn to live, love and lead like Jesus. Then you're on the road to acquiring wisdom.

Keeping Your Mouth Shut

(There is) a time to be silent and a time to speak.

—Ecclesiastes 3:7 NIV

One of the most important bits of advice I can give you is this:

Think
before
you
open
your
mouth
and
say
something.

Now, that should get your attention. I know of no better advice to give you while you are kids and later when you grow up and grow old.

Think about it.

How often do we speak before we have really thought about what we end up saying?

Examples:

I got mad at a guy at school who bullied one of my friends.

"Stop that," I yelled. "Pick on someone you own size."

I had forgotten that the bully was about twice my size and had big fists. The bully turned and started after me. Fortunately, I could run faster than the bully.

I once misbehaved and decided not to tell my parents because I knew I would get a whipping. I had played with matches behind the barn and set a small patch of weeds afire. Luckily, the barn wasn't damaged. I knew, however, that if I opened my mouth and confessed, I might get a licking.

As it turned out, I finally confessed, opened my mouth and began to bawl like a baby. Apparently, mom and dad felt sorry for me and let me off with a good scolding.

Of course, I knew not to open my mouth while chewing food at the table. My mother said this showed bad manners.

Through the years, my parents and teachers suggested how to choose my words and when to speak as I grew up. Unfortunately, I still have trouble because I often open my mouth and speak without thinking.

At other times I find that I should open my moth and say something but don't because I fear that someone will get mad at me and decide to no longer be my friend.

That too often happens when I should say something about Jesus, who told us to "make disciples" as we travel through life. That assignment includes you and me, not just our missionary friends.

If we think about it, Jesus will help us know when it's the right time to tell his story to other girls and boys. Jesus liked children. He liked them so much he died for them. Of course, he rose from the grave and lives again.

That's something you will want to open your mouth and talk about with people you meet, including school-yard bullies.

Feeling Anxious

Do not be anxious about anything, but in every situation, by prayer and petition, with thanksgiving, present your requests to God.

—Philippians 4:6 NIV

I don't care how grown up you are, every person feels anxious on occasion. Being anxious is a lot like being nervous, worried, frightened.

I recall being anxious many times during my lifetime.

For example, I discovered that you have to be on the lookout for ghosts and goblins, especially when you're sleeping alone on the second floor and you hear something scurrying across the floor under your bed. Might be a mouse, or it might be a ghost.

Or when the lightning flashes brilliantly outdoors during a storm, and the thunder booms so loudly that you think the windows will shatter.

I remember when I cut across a neighbor's field, and a bull chased me. I ran lickety split as fast as I could and climbed over the fence seconds before the bull arrived. I tore my pants on the barbed wire, but I escaped.

We're told in the Bible not to be anxious, not to worry, not to dwell on things we cannot control.

That's good advice, but you may find that it doesn't always work. I am still anxious about a lot of things, including whether my favorite sports team will win, whether I may get sick and miss a party or whether I'll miss the bus and be late for an appointment.

So, how should we deal with being anxious, worry and fear?

First, I make a practice of looking at life as a glass filled to the brim with chocolate milk. That way, I don't have to worry where the missing milk might be hiding.

Second, rather than worry, I often start whistling or think of the Mary Poppin's song about "a little bit of sugar makes the medicine go down." Then I remember that mom is going to fix my favorite meal of fried chicken, mashed potatoes and gravy and realize that life doesn't get much better than that.

Third, before I give a speech, I write out the words and practice what I'm going to say. "Two times?" you ask. "No, at least a dozen."

Notice the scripture at the top of the first page reminds us to tell God what's bothering us. It's also okay to ask for some help. Nag God a bit. Explain why you're anxious, nervous or worried. Let God help you deal with the problem.

Also don't overlook thanking God for everything you can think of during the day. That will keep your mind on the positive side of things. I spend more time thanking God than I do praying for things.

And I often thank God for you.

I confess, however, that I once was anxious about one of my great-grandaughters who was going through surgery. She's okay now.

You see, I want her to enjoy a long and adventuresome life like I have, knowing that she will be anxious on occasion but can trust the Lord when the going gets tough.

Making Music

David and all Israel were celebrating before God with all their might, singing songs and playing all kinds of musical instruments—lyres, harps, tambourines, cymbals, and trumpet.

—1 Chronicles 13:8 NIV

I was lucky to have been born into a family of music-makers. My mom played piano. My dad played violin. They met because they were music-makers, were married and reared a family of music-makers.

So, consider yourself fortunate if your folks play something more musical than golf or tennis. If you turn out to be the only music-maker in the family, then go for it because music can turn a downer day into a song.

I suspect the first music you heard after being born was a lullaby your mother sang. Later, she may have taught you to sing "Twinkle Twinkle Little Star." No doubt you sing in Sunday School and in church. Some schools have choirs, which can be a lot of fun, especially if you can read music and sing on key.

I always liked to read the story of King David playing before God "with all his might." That's the way music should be played, especially if you're playing drums or a BIG bass horn.

I played the sousaphone, which is a BIG musical instrument that wraps around your body and ends up as a huge metal disk above your head. You can really OOMPA with one of those things.

But first, you probably should make music with your

voice. It's easy to learn because you probably were born with one. I must confess, however, that some people can't carry a tune. If you are one of those, consider playing the drums. You don't' have to be on key when you bang away on a drum. A lot of kids like to put a lot of drums and cymbals around them and whack away. Make sure, however, that your folks have a basement where you can practice because the neighbors won't like to hear all of the banging.

If you can't sing on key, you might want to learn to play the guitar. You can take a guitar with you to school, to church camps and on vacations and have a lot of fun. However, it's difficult to take drums or a sousaphone anywhere unless you have a BIG truck.

I advise, however, that you first learn to play the piano. I tried to learn how to play with both hands, to read music and to play the piano as well as my mom. Unfortunately, I had trouble learning to play the C scale with both hands and ended up playing chords rather than real music.

I did learn, however, to read music, which made it easy for me to learn how to play the sousaphone. This skill also made it possible for me to sing the baritone parts in choirs in college, in the Air Force and in church.

There's a catch, however. If you want to become a music-maker, you need to practice, practice, practice, and I know how hard it is for you to practice, practice, practice.

If you practice, however, eventually you may be able to make music, the kind that my father played on a violin nearly every day of his life. He loved making music. You will, too.

Crying Real Tears

He will wipe away every tear from their eyes, and death shall be no more, neither shall there be mourning, nor crying, nor pain anymore, for the former things have passed away.

—Revelation 21:4 ESV

Let me say right off the bat that it's okay to cry about anything and about everything. As a baby, you cry because you're hungry, you want attention or you've got a wet diaper.

As you grow up, you learn to cry for various reasons. My brother, who was a teacher, is an expert on crying. I know because students often cry after they see the grades on papers they turn in during class.

My brother reminds us that crying helps babies develop their lungs. As they grow up, they add kicking and hitting to their crying, often to get attention. In other words, you will learn that crying is a form of exercise and communication. That's a big word that means "being heard."

As you become a teenage boy, you learn not to cry when you whack your thumb with a hammer because boys your age don't cry. If you're a girl, you likely will be hugged or kissed if you cry. So, if you want to get the attention of a good-looking guy, cry every chance you get.

My brother points out that crying is used as a defensive and as an offensive weapon. Men are often judged by how well they control grief. Women often are judged by how they grieve when someone hurts their feelings or something bad happens to members of their family and friends.

As a boy, I don't recall crying much. Yeah, I remember

that I cried when I cut a shin bone on my left leg while chopping sassafras brush on our farm. I thought I was going to die because I had to limp a long way home on a bleeding leg. My folks bandaged the wound and told me I was lucky that I didn't cut off my leg. I still carry that scar on my leg, but I no longer cry about it. Normally, when I get a chance today, I pull up my left pant leg and show my scar to people. I tell them that I learned a big lesson about being careful when you're whacking something with a sharp knife.

Today, I often cry tears of joy when someone tells a good joke or pulls a prank on me. I also cry with joy when babies are born and when my favorite football team loses. I don't cry over spilt milk, however, because I drink Slurpees. Now, if you tip over my Slurpee, that's a different matter.

I want to share a story that my brother tells about crying. He is two years younger than me. We used to fight as boys, but we are best friends today.

"I can remember crying several times when I was young," my brother writes. "I can't remember crying later in life. Yes, I cried, but I kept my tears inside. I did not show them.

"This worked well for me until my wife died. Then, I had no way or place to hide them. So, Real Tears came tumbling down. I believe this was the first time my children ever saw me cry.

"I no longer hide real tears, nor am I afraid for others to see them. Some tears are happy and some are sad, but I no longer fear anyone knowing how I really feel. My God knows how I feel, and He is there to help me."

That's good advice for all of us to follow.

Learning to Lose

Whoever tries to keep their life will lose it, and whoever loses their life will preserve it.

—Luke 17:33 NIV

Have you ever been on a team that lost?

Your heart sinks. You may wanna cry. You feel terrible.

I remember the time that I lost while running the half-mile during a track meet when I was a junior in college. I had never lost a race before. As I crossed the finish line in second place, I saw my world collapse around me. Turns out that I later lost a lot of races on the track and in my life.

We're all losers.

Hold on there, you say. It's not nice to talk about losing. We should be lifting one another up, encouraging one another, ignoring the ugly things in our lives.

Well, you had better face the facts. All of us are losers some of the time.

So, how do we deal with losing?

I used to cry, scream, pout, offer excuses, refuse to talk to anyone, especially to my parents. I wanted to soak in my sorrow. I wanted to kick the cat. I wanted to blame my failure on someone else.

Eventually, I got over being disappointed about losing, especially when I learned that mom was serving fried chicken, mashed potatoes and gravy for supper. Where I grew up in Missouri, we called dinner supper. Later, when I moved to Oregon, lunch was served at noon and dinner was served at night. Confusing, ain't it?

Anyway, as I grew up and discovered whiskers growing on my face, I learned how to deal with loss.

I discovered that someone is likely to win and someone is likely to lose during any kind of competition. So, when I lost a race, I didn't spend much time thinking about something I couldn't change. Rather, I tried to figure out how I could be more successful in the future.

But what about the little things? You know, spilling a glass of milk? Tripping over an elephant? Wrecking your bike? Being late for class? Getting an answer wrong during a test? Receiving a grade card with nothing but C's on it? Hitting a wrong note during a piano recital?

These examples describe how we often can't help but lose. I call spilling milk an accident. It also reminds me that I should pay attention the next time that I pick up a glass of milk. If I want to get good grades, I need to spend more time and effort in studying rather than playing electronic games.

Some things in life are more important than others. In case you are interested, I suggest that you can learn how to win by doing at least six things:

1. Wash your hands before you eat.
2. Learn to read.
3. Learn how to ride a bike.
4. Learn how to smile.
5. Touch all your bases.
6. Walk with Jesus.

Picking Your Heroes

Don't let anyone deceive you in any way...

—2 Thessalonians 2:3 NIV

We all "look up to" someone. That person often is called a hero. Actually, most of us have several heroes, people we might want to be like when we grow up.

One of my heroes was Stan Musial, a professional baseball player, who played in the outfield for the St. Louis Cardinals starting in 1941. He was called "Stan the Man" when we listened to games on the radio. My hero batted .331 and is considered one of the most consistent hitters in baseball history.

Stan had an unusual batting stance, and although he batted left-handed, I tried to bat like he did even though I was right-handed. Turned out that it worked for me while I played softball in high school.

I figured that Stan was a regular fellow who you not only could count on when hitting, but also when he was off the diamond. He was courteous, stayed out of trouble and served his country in the Navy. He also knew how to play the harmonica. Lived to be 92 years old.

I also had another hero, my mom. She grew up on a farm, worked in the fields and decided to get a college education during a time when women had few career choices. After my brother and I finished high school, she became a teacher. I haven't met anyone with more "true grit" than my mother. She also was loving and kind, except when I misbehaved or failed to practice the piano. Because of people like my mom, women can pick anything they want to do today. So, she's another of my heroes.

So, what are you looking for in a hero? You want someone who is strong? brave? good looking? young? a winner?

Yeah, we're looking for a perfect person. Of course, that's too bad because that means I wouldn't qualify to be your hero. I'm too old. I'm losing my hair. My face is wrinkled. I find it hard to bend over and pick up stuff I spill on the floor. I watch too much television. I'm hard of hearing, and sometimes I forget your name.

That may be why young people these days are so interested in fantasy and science fiction. We can make up perfect heroes. You know, beautiful women who can fly through the air and rescue handsome guys in some outer-world kingdom. Or read about how Cinderella lost a glass slipper and found a Prince to love.

I've only discovered one perfect hero. Turns out he wouldn't win any awards today in Hollywood. He wasn't good looking, didn't play sports, walked around the country giving speeches, treated women and children like they were special, healed the sick, brought dead folks back to life.

A lot of people wanted to make my hero a king, but he didn't want to be one in this world. He said he would be a king later in a perfect world, one where I—and everyone else—could live forever.

All I had to do was follow him.

It's okay to have several heroes in this world. My only advice is not to expect them to be perfect. Be sure, however, to pick people who you can trust and who you like well enough to model your life after.

A person like my friend.

Exploring Choices

Going Fishing

"Come, follow me," Jesus said, "and I will send you out to fish for people."

—Mark 1:17 NIV

I remember the first time I fished. It was on the Finley River in southern Missouri not far from our farm home. I was about 12 years old at the time. It was a summer day, and I fished with a bamboo pole, a bobber, a line and a hook threaded with an earthworm dug from the manure pile behind the barn.

I sat on a large root of a tree beside the river not far from the Lindenlure dam. The river ran slowly there, and I picked a pool of standing water, which means that it wasn't moving. I swung my hook, line and bobber into that pool and waited.

The bobber didn't move for a long time. I wondered whether fish swam in that part of the river and continued to wait. Then the bobber bobbed and went underwater. I yanked a fish out of the river and onto the bank. It turned out to be a small sunfish, and I tossed it back into the river.

Now, catching my first fish was something that I'll never forget, not even if I live to be 159 years old. What I will remember is that my dad took me fishing and that he was there when I caught the fish.

You will learn that it's important to have a father beside you wherever you go in this world. Some of you have earthly fathers who take you fishing, to ball games, to piano practice and to school. I hope that all of you also invite a heavenly father to accompany you throughout your earthly life. Both fathers are important, especially the heavenly father who never leaves you even after you grow up and leave home.

I've got to tell you a couple of other stories about my earthly father, the guy I remember as a farmer, as a musician and as a fisherman.

My father, who was your great-great-grandad, wasn't much of a success as a farmer. He picked the job only because he married a farmer's daughter, who had access to a 160-acre wheat ranch. Later, the Great Depression and dust storms drove them to the Ozark Hills in southern Missouri.

I never once heard my father complain about "hard times." I never once heard my father swear. I did, however, hear my father play a violin nearly every night before I grew up and left home. Later, when I became a father, I took our four children fishing. A son became especially good at fishing, especially fly-fishing. You tie a make-believe fly on the end of the line rather than thread a worm on a hook when you fly-fish. My son also became an expert fly-tier, which is someone who creates all kinds of bugs that are supposed to attract fish.

I joined him by learning to fly-fish and to tie flies. Even though I practiced and practiced tying flies, I never was good at it. My son, however, patted me on my balding head and offered a word of encouragement.

"Your flies should catch fish," he said. "Fish often like the kind of fly you tie because they look like they're injured."

So, I picked up my flies and joined him on another fishing outing.

I pray that your father takes you fishing.

Building Character

So, God created male and female in his own image....

—Genesis 1:27

Christians believe that they are to act like God, which means that they are loving, joyful, patient, kind, good, faithful, gentle and don't get time-outs for not towing the line.

I don't know about you, but that's a tall order for anyone to measure up to, especially all of the time.

Of course, the word, character, has other meanings. For example, you may have played make-believe and acted as though you were someone else. I like to write stories about make-believe people who face dragons and other scary characters.

And don't forget people who act out parts in plays on stage. You probably have acted like someone else before an audience. That happens, too, in movies that you see in theaters and on television screens.

That's not so unusual. A lot of people—kids and grown-ups—want to be like someone else, especially their heroes. Take for example, the guy who likes a football player so much that he begins to wear a shirt with the football player's number on it.

Or someone who gets carried away and begins to look and to act like that person, maybe by playing a guitar, singing in a shaky voice and wobbling his knees and hips around. You may have heard about such a guy. His name was Elvis Presley. He's not shaking anything now.

Then there's your great-grandad, who sometimes is called

a character, probably because he acts silly, says and does outrageous things that someone as old as he is normally doesn't say and do.

Okay, back to the God thing. You will discover that it's hard to keep track of all the things we ought to be and do if we're going to act like we should.

For example, you're great-grandad doesn't always love everyone he meets. Some folks are downright mean and unlovable.

And I'm not always joyful, especially when I don't get my way. Which reminds me about the times I wouldn't let my brother play with my toys. I wasn't gentle or self-controlled. I let him know that he wasn't to put his hands on my things. They were mine, mine, mine, mine.

During the past 80 years, I figured out that each person is different from everyone else. That's the way God made us. Some of us are smart and want to be in charge. We want to lead. We want to be in the center of action. Other kids may be as smart but are more easy-going. They don't talk so much because they like to listen, to test the water. In other words, each one of us has what is called a different personality.

As you grow up, you will decide whether you want to be a person who is loving, who stands by your family and friends, who is honest, who respects someone who is different than you.

These are blocks that God gives us to build character. Just don't expect to complete the task while you're a kid.

Saying, 'I Love You'

For this is the message that you have heard from the beginning, that we should love one another.

—1 John 3:11 ESV

It's easy to love someone. It's often hard, however, to tell someone, "I love you."

Yeah, I get it. When we're in grade school, we often think that saying "I love you" is something two people tell one another a couple of weeks before they get married.

At least that was what I thought when I was growing up on a farm and my only playmates were boys.

I finally fell in love during third grade. At least I was teased about being sweet on a girl because we both never missed a spelling word and scored a hundred percent on all of our tests. I was so shy that I never spoke to this girl who sat two rows away from me in the classroom, and I never went near her on the playground.

I've told you about the year I attended a one-room school during fifth grade. All of the boys—six of us—fell in love with an eighth-grade girl who often walked to and from school with us. She smelled nice of perfume and told us all sorts of romantic stuff. Things like hugging and kissing. Then one day she disappeared. Ran off with a guy who drove a new car.

Well, there's romantic love, and there are other kinds of love.

I'm thinking about the times that I sing the "Star Spangled Banner" and "America the Beautiful" during sports events and when I say "The Pledge of Allegiance." Goose bumps pop up on my body, and I sometimes get tears in my eyes. Yeah, great-grandads can get weepy.

You will learn to appreciate how fortunate you are to live in a country where you enjoy so much freedom to say what you want to say and to do what you want to do. Of course, it helps if you love rather than hate people.

When I was growing up, I knew that my mom and dad loved me because of the way they treated me. They listened when I got mad and when I threw a fit. They encouraged me when I took off on some crazy adventure. They attended my ball games and school events.

But my parents never told me, "I love you." In those days people just didn't talk that way. Actually, many parents don't tell their kids they love them today.

So, a few years ago, I decided to begin telling my children, their children and now you, my great-grandchildren, that "I love you" every chance I get. Know, what? They now tell me that they love me. And I believe they mean it.

You need to know that someone else loves you and tells you so—if you will listen. I met Jesus when I was a kid and discovered that he loves me so much that he paid for all of my sins a long time ago. I decided to follow him and told him I was sorry for sinning so much.

It's a great comfort to know that I'll walk FOREVER with my friend because he loves me with no strings attached. The last time I checked, FOREVER is a very, very, very long time.

WATCHING WHAT YOU WATCH

"Therefore keep watch because you do not know on what day your Lord will come.

—Matthew 24:42 NIV

You're going to get a lot of heat about what to watch and what not to watch while you're a kid.

Your folks could simplify this if they got rid of the television set(s) and refuse to let you look at any hand-held device other than a baseball bat or a book.

When I was a kid, television hadn't been invented. Our farm didn't have electricity. So, the only time we got to listen to the radio was when we took the battery out of the car and moved it into the living room. We only had enough juice in the battery to listen to the "Green Hornet" once a week.

So, without television, Facebook, tweeting and stuff like that, what did we do during our spare time when we were kids?

During the school year, we finished our homework.

Then we played games. You know, stuff like checkers. When we got bored playing board games we got as Christmas gifts, we made up our own, which took a bit of imagination. I still remember the game I made up. I rolled teams of different colored marbles back and forth in a cardboard box. The marble that ended up in a corner, won a point for that team.

We also played music. My mom played the piano, my dad played the violin and I sang. Songs like "She'll Be Coming 'Round the Mountain" and "Swing Low." Sometimes neighbors dropped in and joined us. One woman played a guitar and another played a bass that she made out of a wash tub.

Of course, when we had spare time during the evenings, we often read. Dad usually read the Bible, mom read all sorts of books and I read adventure stories. I could join the heroes and travel with them to far away places like Shangri-La, the South Seas and the Klondike.

Well, you live in a more modern world. You have lots of things you can watch during the day, after school and during the weekend. The other day I saw a tiny kid in a baby stroller who was playing with what looked like a TV screen about the size of a slice of bread.

A recent study found that 24 percent of teenagers go online "almost constantly" and that some kids take their mobile devices to bed with them.

Wow, and they watch them during meals and even during school.

So, what's fair when your folks tell you not to watch your mobile devices during dinner or while you should be sleeping? Or restrict your TV watching to an hour or so a day? Do you cry? pout? raise a fuss? accuse your parents of being unfair because your friends get to spend all the time they want with mobile devices?

Shape up and figure you're lucky if your folks don't dump your TV set and all of the other electronic gadgets into the garbage can and suggest that you spend more time reading, playing real games, doing your chores, walking your dog. Stuff like that.

In any event, I figure that I was lucky as a kid because after I helped milk the cows, feed the horses, gather the eggs, work in the garden and slop the hogs, I was all tuckered out and went to bed.

Being Religious

For God so loved the world that he gave his one and only Son, that whoever believes in him shall not perish but have eternal life.

—John 3:16 NIV

I pray that all of you choose to follow Jesus, but that may not happen.

Surprised?

No, I'm just being honest because some of you may follow other gods. I hope, however, that you give Jesus a chance. Otherwise, you will be missing out on a sure bet.

But I don't gamble, you argue.

Sure, you do, and depending on any other friend than Jesus is like jumping out of a rocket without a parachute.

Or, so I believe.

You've probably heard my story. So, I'll tell it to you again.

When I was a boy, I lived on a farm, and we only had one church to pick from. It was in a one-room building across the road from a one-room school.

My family didn't attend church because our church was located in town, and we didn't have money enough to buy gas to get there. However, when I was about 10 years old, I attended a series of revival meetings in the church across from the school with my buddy Harold.

Each night during the revival we sat on the front row. Otherwise, Harold and I couldn't see what was going on. All I remember is that the minister became quite exited and thumped on a Bible while talking about being saved from going to hell. The catch was: You had to accept Christ as your savior to get there.

As you know, I can get rather excited on occasion. My buddy also became fidgety sitting there on that hard, wood bench. So, when the preacher invited us sinners to follow Jesus, Harold and I jumped up and went forward.

It's been so long ago that I can't remember the details, but I felt saved. So did Harold. He took being saved so seriously he eventually became a preacher. I became a writer, got married, had four kids, eight grandkids and now a passel of great-grandkids. You're one of them.

That brings us to my thoughts about becoming a Christian. I can only speak for myself, but I believe that I'm going to be following Jesus throughout what they call eternity.

Now, I can't tell you how long eternity may be because I'm not there yet. That is, unless I've died since sharing this advice with you. But I'm certain that I've made the right choice.

I believe what that preacher said during that revival so many years ago. He said that I've been saved. He said that my sins won't be held against me when I die because Jesus paid the penalty. All I had to do was to accept his invitation, to confess my sins and to follow Him.

I pray that you will choose to follow Jesus because I want to be with you in heaven. Otherwise, I believe that you'll be in hot water. Real hot water.

Discovering the Birds and the Bees

Adam and his wife were both naked, and they felt no shame.

—Genesis 2:25 NIV

I had an advantage of learning about "the birds and the bees" as a farm boy. In case your parents are too timid to explain, we're talking about the sexual act.

Horses do it. Cows do it. Sheep do it. Even birds and bees do it. Otherwise, how do you explain how babies are made? Keep in mind, however, that your parents may believe that if they describe "what comes naturally," you might do it before you're married.

So, let's talk sex.

One of the reasons you "have to be home by 10 p.m." as a teenager is that your parents know that kissing and hugging often take place after you have attended a social or school function with your boyfriend or girlfriend and that kissing and hugging may lead to "something else."

It's the "something else" I want to discuss with you.

Before I do, let me explain that one of the reasons some parents school their kids at home is to prevent them from hearing "bad stuff" on the school grounds, including talk about "the birds and the bees."

Now that I have you all worked up and interested in what I have to say about "the birds and bees," we'll take a time-out. You know what a time-out is: Time to let your parents get their tempers in check and time to figure out what to say and to do when you misbehave.

After taking a time-out, I realized that your parents probably are reading this chapter before you do. So, I'll address my thoughts to them rather than to you. Why? Because it is critical that parents rather than someone else talk to you about sex.

So, what might parents tell their children about sex?

Tell them about the unique features of the body and why God designed it that way and start the discussion when you introduce them to Dick and Jane.

Tell them how babies are made.

Tell them how boys and girls can prevent becoming pregnant before the time when they can become pregnant.

And talk to them about masturbation and pornography. These topics are issues among people of all ages.

Don't use the excuse that "if my children know how to prevent having babies, they will begin having sex before marriage." Poor philosophy. (That's like saying: "If my children don't know about sin, they won't sin.) And have you talked about the flip side of "the birds and bees" equation? Maybe suggest that your child read the Song of Solomon.

Granted, your religious belief and practice figure into the equation, but with the growth of social media, nothing remains secret long, including a generation of children who are connected electronically to the universe.

If you, the parent, want your daughter or son to be chaste before marriage, then don't keep "the birds and the bees" a secret. As a great-grandparent, I know it's no secret at any age.

Falling in Love

You shall love the LORD your God with all your heart, with all your soul and with all your mind.

—Matthew 22:37 NIV

You can fall in love with a lot of things when you're a kid. I fell in love with writing when I was 5 years old and have been putting words on paper for more than 80 years.

I also fell in love with bike riding and spent hours exploring the countryside on two wheels. As I've told you before, we didn't wear helmets in those days. But I was an expert rider, and I never had a wreck.

I fell in love with a girl in the third grade, but I was too bashful to talk to her. So, that love affair didn't go anywhere. As a fifth grader I fell in love with an eighth grader who ran off with a guy who showed up at her place with a new car. Eventually, I met your great-grandma, and we've been together for more than 65 years. Now, that's a love affair that would take several chapters to describe.

Through the years I have watched girls and boys fall in love with sports and spend all of their spare time playing baseball, softball, soccer and stuff like that. Others fell in love with music. Today, a lot of kids fall in love with computer games.

I find nothing wrong with falling in love with people and things. The good Lord made us that way. After all, we need to explore what we want to do in life and who we want to spend our time with.

While you're at it, check out where you want to spend eternity, which is a looooooong time. In other words: forever.

Now, I don't know about you, but when I was a boy, I figured out that no one else was looking out of my body, which made me special. You are special, too. So, who are you, and why are you here on earth?

Many books have been written about this topic, but I've only read one that makes any sense. Lots of folks believe that if they're good enough, they will live forever. But how good do you have to be to be good enough? is the question that always pops up in my mind. Who sets the standard?

The book I follow tells about a man who lived a perfect life, died on a cross and rose from the dead. His name is Jesus, and I chose to follow his teachings when I was a kid like you. Why? Because I didn't find any other person who lived a perfect life and who promised to forgive all of the things I've done wrong if I decided to follow him.

My advice is: Check out the gods of this world because your eternal welfare is at stake. It doesn't matter whether your parents follow or believe in Jesus. One of these days you will be old enough to make your own choice. I promise that you will fall in love with Jesus if you really look for him. He's always near whether you're good or bad. You can talk to him at any time. Tell him what's bothering you and thank him for the good things in your life. Like candy bars.

What's at stake?

A life worth living in this world and the next.

It's called eternity.

Finding a Spouse

Do not be unevenly yoked…

—2 Corinthians 6:14 ESV

One of the most important decisions you will make in life is deciding whom to marry.

On one hand, it may be the easiest decision you will make. On the other, it may be the most difficult.

Let me explain.

First, the good Lord wired us so that we're attracted physically to members of the opposite sex. As a boy, I knew who the good-looking girls were in my third-grade class. They got prettier the older they got, especially when they filled out in the right places, smiled those pretty smiles and looked my way. I'm not a girl. So, I don't know what girls see in boys, but they tend to enjoy going to dances, to movies, that sort of stuff—with boys.

By the time you can get a driver's license, you're ready to settle down, go steady, maybe sneak a kiss or two, hold hands, that sort of thing. Eventually, you end up with someone you like so much you think about that person all of the time and want to spend all of your time with that person.

First thing you know, you want to get married and to live happily ever after with that person. That's what I mean by finding a spouse.

Keep in mind that more than half of the people who find a spouse fail to stay with that spouse. They get divorced, leave one another, find another spouse.

If you're interested in sticking with your first spouse, listen up. I have some words of advice:

First, pick a spouse who believes in the same things you believe in, especially important things like heaven and hell. Don't be unevenly yoked.

Second, promise to court your spouse every day for the rest of your married life. This promise may become more difficult, especially when babies arrive and your focus shifts to taking care of them. If you fail to think of your spouse as special, the two of you may end up strangers after the children grow up and leave the house.

Third, before you get married, ask these questions: Will I still love this person when this person's hair turns gray, when I have to push that person around in a wheelchair, when that person sometimes forgets my name?

You know that lots of people these days are living together without being married. I'm not going to say whether that is the right or wrong way to live, but I don't advise that you pick a spouse that way.

I do know, however, that the Bible says that we should not pull apart what God has put together. Fortunately, I found a spouse who has stuck with me more than 65 years.

I like to tell the story about how we met. She was wearing brown-and-white saddle shoes the day she swept down a line of college students, laughing and flirting with all the guys. As I looked up from her shoes to her pretty legs, up her slender body and saw her pretty smile, I was a gonner. I still see that pretty smile every time I look into her face today.

Communicating

The Lord is near to all who call on him, to all who call on him in truth.

—Psalms 145:18 NIV

When you are riding in the back seat of the car and you see an ice cream shop ahead, you beg your mom or dad to stop and buy you an ice cream cone.

That's what communicating means. It's a message you can send by talking, by writing, by shouting, by jumping up and down, by pouting, by crying, by laughing. In other words, you're letting someone know how you feel or think about something.

For example, newborn babies often cry to let moms know that they're hungry or that they want a diaper changed. It's a way of letting someone else know how you feel or what you believe.

I remember that when I was about eight years old, I became upset with my parents. They were spending much more time with my younger brother and giving him too much attention. I was jealous although I didn't know what that meant when I was eight years old.

So, I told my father about why I was unhappy and sulked so much. He admitted that he and my mother were spending more time and paying more attention to my brother because he had been real sick, almost died. My father said he and my mother loved me as much as my brother and said he was sorry that I felt they had been unfair.

As you grow up, you will learn that communicating often

is more difficult than you may want to admit.

For example, you may feel that a teacher treats you unfairly, gives you bad grades, marks up your papers more than other students, asks you more difficult questions than other students.

That's the way I felt in fourth grade. My teacher marked up my papers, pointed out mistakes I made with punctuation and with how I put sentences together. I finally got up enough gumption to ask the teacher why she was picking on me. Her answer: because you have great potential as a writer, and you need to learn how to write.

Wow, that was communication. It wasn't something I wanted to hear, but something that I needed to hear. It also inspired me to learn where to put commas and how to write sentences.

I also needed to learn and to be reminded often that I communicate by smiling, laughing, pouting, crying, how I listen or don't listen. For example, I always perk up when someone mentions ice cream. If someone suggests that it's time to clean up my room, I immediately begin pouting.

Isn't it amazing that we're sending messages every minute, every hour, every day in what we think, in what we say and in what we do or don't do

It's even more amazing that you and I have a friend who knows how we feel and what we need every second of our lives. A friend who laughs and cries with us, who understands us, who cares for us and who loves us no matter what. That's the friend I've been communicating with since I met Jesus.

Dealing With Color

I have set my rainbow in the clouds, and it will be the sign of the covenant between me and the earth.

—Genesis 9:13 NIV

Rainbows are beautiful reminders of how we are loved by a creator who uses color to decorate the place where we live.

Nevertheless, color will create a lot of challenges during your lifetime. At least it has for me. And how you deal with color will paint much of your life's story.

I can only speak from my experience, so here it is:

Red has been my favorite since I began coloring outside the lines in color books that my parents and friends gave to me as birthday and Christmas gifts. I always wore out the red before the yellow, which is kinda puny.

I suppose I like red because it stands out, makes a statement, says "wake up."

Santa Claus wears a red suit. So, I figure that wearing red pants should be okay for grown-ups to wear on special occasions. I wore red pants once, but folks laughed and thought I was being a bit of a show-off. I could have worn white pants, but you can't wrestle in the mud wearing that color. Well, maybe you can wrestle in the mud, but you shouldn't wear white when you do.

There's a flip side to red. For example, I often picked a red crayon to color a fire in a color book. I remember going to a lot of fires and writing stories about them while I was a newspaper reporter. Fire often damaged and destroyed buildings. People in the buildings and fire fighters often were hurt. Some died.

I learned that colors may mean different things to different people at different times. Red is great when I think about eating a cold slice of watermelon but not so good when I'm handed a second-place red ribbon when I really wanted to win the first-place blue ribbon in a race at school.

As you know, the color of our skin can cause a lot of trouble. You probably live in a world where your friends are black, white and brown. You're lucky because my friends were all white while I was growing up.

I didn't meet a person who was any color but white until I finished six years of college. Later, I joined the Air Force where I trained with several black guys and a dozen fellows whose ancestors were Polish. All of them were among the funniest and friendliest guys I have ever known.

Of course, not all of the people I meet are funny and friendly. Some are downright mean and nasty. Some are white. Some are black. Some are brown. I would rather that we all have red skin. Remember, red is my favorite color.

I don't know why people get upset when they meet someone who isn't wearing the same color skin. I didn't get to choose the color of my skin. Neither did you.

So, don't judge a person by the color of skin that person is wearing.

Picture that person as a rainbow.

And remember who painted the sky with all those beautiful colors.

Seeking Adventure

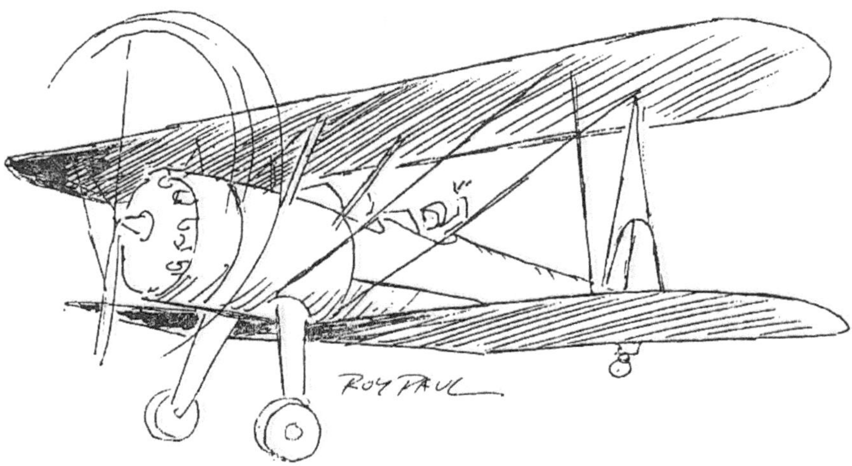

Taking a Risk

Enter by the narrow gate. For the gate is wide and the way is easy that leads to destruction, and those who enter by it are many. For the gate is narrow and the way is hard that leads to life, and those who find it are few.

—Matthew 7:13-14 ESV

When big folks talk about taking a risk, they really are trying to figure out whether they may get hurt or lose something. Too often, they fail to look on the sunny side of life.

An example:

Clouds sail across the sky. So, we won't go camping today because it may rain. (Guess what? We went camping. It rained for a few minutes, but we had a great time. Dad caught a fish, mom read a book and I picked a bunch of wild flowers and saw a deer.)

Another example:

I may make a mistake and embarrass myself before an audience. So, I won't try. (Guess what? I practiced my solo, played it during the concert and the audience gave me a standing ovation.)

This is not to say that things always turn out for the best. Sometimes when we take a risk, we fail. Keep in mind, however, that we often learn more when we fail than when we succeed.

When I was a boy, it took me about two weeks before I could play the C scale with one hand on a piano. The risk of failure wasn't too high, and I didn't risk getting hurt or losing something. The reward was out in front of me because I eventually learned how to play the C scale with both hands—at the same time. (My teacher gave me a gold star for that. Wow. Life doesn't get much better than a gold star.)

All of this suggests that we take risks all the time, but we need to give serious thought about taking BIG risks. You know, the decisions that may cause us to lose something valuable or to hurt us but that also offer the chance of success and happiness.

Years ago your great-grandma and I calculated the risk involved in moving from southern Missouri to Oregon with a 2-year-old daughter and a 6-month-old son. We packed all we owned in a small trailer and car and headed to the Pacific Northwest without a job and with only $300. Taking the risk paid off BIG TIME. We found a beautiful state, a home and a job. If we had not taken the risk, you great-grandkids may have been Missouri tigers rather than Oregon ducks.

You will find that risks come in small, medium and large sizes. You won't have to spend much time thinking about the small and medium risks, but don't let the possibility of being hurt or losing something stop you from trying to reach a goal.

When it comes to taking a risk, I trust in the Lord, knowing that I'll be in good hands no matter whether I fail or succeed. Jesus took the greatest risk anyone can take and won. So, walk with Jesus.

Liking Your Work

So I decided there is nothing better than to enjoy food and drink and to find satisfaction in work. Then I realized that these pleasures are from the hand of God.

—Ecclesiastes 2:24 NLT

"Find something you want to do as a trade or a profession. Then do it to the best of your ability," my parents advised my brother and me when we were boys.

That decision wasn't hard for me. I decided I wanted to be a writer when I was a kid, and I've written about a zillion words during the past 80 years.

It's often been hard work to gather information and to write newspaper stories when I was a journalist and then later to write books like this one.

But I love being a writer.

The happiest people I know love what they do. The farmer who gets up early to plow a field, to milk cows, to take care of chores. The banker who enjoys working with numbers and with people. The person who cleans a house and prepares meals.

I can't speak for everyone, but I have found that happy people often view their jobs as important, even if they are doing what is called "grunt" work. You know, stuffing burgers in a bun and serving them with a cold drink and fries. Over and over again. How do I know they enjoy their work?

Here are a few clues:

The person looks forward to going to work on Monday morning. The person smiles a real smile rather than a fake one on the job. The person who doesn't complain about his or her boss or about being unappreciated or underpaid.

I've got to tell you a story about an important lesson I learned when I began working in a print shop while in junior high. I was paid ten cents an hour as I learned the printing trade. I once complained to my supervisor, saying, "Did you know that I only make ten cents an hour?" He replied: "Are you worth it?"

That about rounds up what I want to say about enjoying your work. You see, what you do in life may be more important and more worthwhile than you realize. You may put a smile on someone's face, give someone hope, inspire someone to do a good job because you are doing your level best, and you're not whining while you work.

You soon will discover that too many people complain about their work, about their boss, about how they are treated. That's not what the author of Ecclesiastes had in mind about enjoying your life.

I recall that I spent a summer as a boy picking strawberries for a penny a box. I got sunburned even though I wore a straw hat. I could have been swimming with my friends or reading a book in the shade.

I watched how other people picked strawberries, and figured out how to pick real fast without bruising the strawberry. I knew how important that job was to me because I finally saved enough pennies to buy a toy typewriter. Hey, I was a writer, and I needed a typewriter.

Volunteering Is a Sticky Business

As each has received a gift, use it to serve one another as good stewards of God's varied grace.

—1 Peter 4:10 ESV

Volunteers often are praised, honored and respected. Be warned, however, because volunteering can be a sticky business.

First, we know that we should "serve one another." Be careful, however. If you get too much ice cream piled on a cone, it's likely to thaw and begin running down your hand and arm.

I must agree that most of us need help during our lifetime when things get out of hand. I'm thinking about a person who has had a bad stroke of luck or has lost a loved one.

I remember the time when I was a boy. A neighbor fell and suffered a broken leg during harvest season. My father and all our neighbors were working day and night cutting and threshing wheat, but all of us volunteered to make sure that our neighbor's wheat was harvested.

I also remember when a boyhood friend of mine got a real sharp pain in his side, and the pain wouldn't go away. For some reason, it took too much time to get my friend to the hospital, and he died after his appendix ruptured. The whole community turned out to supply food to the boy's parents, to do their farm chores and to hug and love them.

It's rather clear that sometimes we not only should but

also want to volunteer, to help our family, friends and community. However, that doesn't give us an excuse for not doing our chores or our school work.

Here's something I learned about volunteering: Think before you act.

I got into trouble when I was in the fifth grade. The teacher talked about how great it would be if we had a class party to celebrate Columbus Day. I was so excited that I told the teacher that my parents could help with the party. BIG mistake. When I told my parents that I had volunteered their help, they explained that they already had plans for that day and could not help with the party.

So, I was embarrassed and felt like a dirty dog when I told the teacher that we would have to celebrate Columbus without my parents.

Later, I made the mistake of trying to please the sergeant in charge of my training after I joined the Air Force. He wanted someone to volunteer to help with what he called "a very important job." That sounded cool to me because I wanted to be needed, helpful, popular. So, without knowing what the important job was, I volunteered and spent my free time helping clean bathrooms for a week. At that point of my life I vowed to find out what's involved before I volunteer for anything.

I know that we're encouraged to help other folks when they have real needs. Make sure, however, that those needs are real and that you have time to meet those needs.

So, don't expect me to walk your dog, clean your bathroom or take care of your stuff unless you've suffered a broken arm or are hospitalized with a sore thumb.

Today, I'm too busy to walk your dog or to clean your bathroom. I'm going fishing. Want to volunteer to tag along?

Observing the Rule of Three

The heart of man plans his way, but the Lord establishes his steps.

—Proverbs 16:9 ESV

"Oh, another rule?" you say. "I'm getting tired of listening to rules. Why don't we talk about baseball or ice cream? What's so important about this Rule of Three?"

First, let me tell you where I heard about this rule, and why I believe that it's important.

I listened to an advertising executive talk about the rule one summer in Charleston, S.C. (Meanwhile, your great-grandma and your grandparents played in the ocean. Talk about life being unfair.)

Anyway, this advertising big shot said he once owned a business. As he made friends in the community, he started to volunteer for all sorts of good causes. You know, the chamber of commerce, a service club, a business organization, etc., etc., etc.

"I became so busy working as a volunteer that my business nearly went bankrupt," he said. "So, I sold my business, got a different job and began following the Rule of Three."

Each year he decides the three most important things in his life other than his job and doesn't add other things to the list. One he calls a major. The other two are minors. So, figure out where and what you want to do with your spare time during the week and on weekends. Don't count sleeping, eating and going to the bathroom. We're talking about the time over which you have some control.

The most important thing you probably do during the winter is to attend some sort of school. That's your job. Now for the Rule of Three. The next most important thing may be learning to play a musical instrument or learning how to play baseball or softball.

Now, you have two minor things to choose other than eating, keeping your room clean and brushing your teeth. If you are in school, completing homework probably is No. 2. If you are a member of a non-school or church group, that could be counted as No. 3.

The Rule of Three permits you to drop an activity and to replace it with something else. The key, of course, is not to add activities to your schedule. You know, a friend begs you to try out for a tiddlywink team. Another friend wants you to become a Scout. Another friend begs you to play banjo in a band. The list can grow bigger and bigger.

In my case, writing is my job. I write books like this one during the day Monday through Friday. I also help cook meals, clean the carpets and work in the yard and garden. That takes most of my time during the day. My No. 1 activity is meeting with a group of guys one morning a week to discuss how God is working in our lives. No. 2 is exercising during the day rather than sitting in front of a TV. No. 3 is fly-fishing. Yes, I may be an old man and have trouble wading a mountain stream, but I still enjoy tying a fly on the line and trying to catch a trout.

If I add something to my schedule, I cut back on the least important of my Rule of Three activities. Unfortunately, that usually means that I don't get to watch TV or to drink Slurpees, but life ain't always fair.

Watching Where You Walk

Yea, though I walk through the valley of the shadow of death, I will fear no evil: for thou art with me; thy rod and thy staff they comfort me.

—Psalms 23:4 KJV

Kids in the United States need not worry about stepping on a bomb when they go for a walk. Kids in other parts of the world aren't so lucky.

When I was a boy, I had to watch where I walked for a lot of reasons.

First, I didn't want to step on a snake, and we had a lot of those poisonous critters on the farm where I lived.

Second, when I milked the cows, I didn't want to step on a pile of manure. If you live on a farm, you have to watch out for those things.

I remember the night I was so scared that I couldn't move. I didn't want to walk anywhere. Actually I wanted to hide under the bed. That happened when I was about 5 years old. The car my parents were driving got stuck in the mud. Water was rising in the creek between the car and our house. Dad couldn't carry my mother, brother and me to the house at the same time. So, he made two trips. He picked me up, carried me across the creek to the house and left me on the back porch.

Lightning flashed across the sky, and thunder boomed like a BIG bass drum. I was terrified. I was so scared that I couldn't move. Meanwhile, my father picked up my mother and younger brother on the second trip, and we all dried our clothes in front of a wood stove.

Your great-grandad also found a lot of good places to walk while he was growing up on the farm.

My favorite walk was to the river to fish with my dad. All we caught were sun perch, but we didn't mind. We just enjoyed watching the bobber on our lines and wishing a fish would pull it under.

I also enjoyed walking to and from school when I was in the fifth grade. I could dream about things I wanted to do and places where I wanted to go when I grew up. I know that it isn't safe for you to walk to school today, but you can do a lot of dreaming about places you want to visit while riding on a bus or in a car.

I did a lot of walking and talking with my buddies while growing up. We sometimes got into trouble, but mostly we made up games to play and things to do together.

The important thing to remember is to think about where you want to walk before you start walking. Figure out in advance whether it is worth your time and effort to get there.

Even though you are careful where you walk during your lifetime, some trails will lead through some scary places. It will be like walking through dark and lonesome valleys.

The best advice I can offer is to walk with a friend you can trust.

I picked a friend to walk with who knows all about the thunder, lightning, snakes and other scary stuff. He walks on water, turns water into wine, heals the sick and brings dead people back to life.

He also created the places where I walk. So, I figured he can and will lead me through dark valleys as well as in the sunlight.

Protecting Your Freedom

For you have been called to live in freedom, my brothers and sisters. But don't use your freedom to satisfy your sinful nature. Instead, use your freedom to serve one another in love

—Galatians 5:13 NLT

It's important for you to know how important freedom really is. I'm not talking about being free to do what you want to do. I'm talking about the freedom we enjoy as citizens of the United States of America.

You will learn a lot about our country's history while growing up. That's great, but it's more important to learn how government works and how important it is for you and for me to help protect our freedom.

For example, members of your family may have served in the armed forces and fought to keep our country free. Others may have served what is called "the public good" by voting and by taking an interest in local, state and federal governmental activities.

First, they vote on issues and on candidates for office. In some states, it has been difficult and sometimes impossible for some people to vote in local, state and federal elections. In other states, you have to stand in line for hours and prove that you are a citizen and that you have a right to vote. In Oregon, ballots are mailed to us before an election, and we aren't rushed into making decisions about issues and candidates for office.

So, beware when you find out that people have trouble voting in the state where you live. But make sure you vote every chance you get. If you don't vote, then you don't deserve to enjoy this freedom we're talking about.

The second thing you need to do is to learn how city, state and federal governments work and to learn about people who run for political offices and how well they serve what is called "the public interest."

Now, here's the rub. Most of us don't want to get involved in politics. Some folks think of politics as dirty and that our public servants only serve their own interests.

So, what do you do about it? First, you quit bellyaching and get to work. You don't have to run for office. You can serve on a government committee, attend city government meetings, get to know your local, state and federal representatives and the issues they deal with.

Freedom is complicated because we have to lose some of our freedom to be free in what is called a representative form of government like we enjoy. In other words, we're not free to do everything we want to do. We need to remember the other person should have the same rights as we do to enjoy living in this country.

So, we pass laws to protect the freedom of everyone. This means that we try to give everyone a "break" when it comes to things like freedom to attend school, to not be picked on when we're at work and to go to any church and to follow any god we choose.

I know that this sounds a bit complicated, but remember two things: First, learn how government works, especially how it spends the taxes you pay. Two, spend some time learning about issues and candidates that appear on a ballot and then VOTE.

Better yet, get involved. Run for office. Become president.

Reaching for the Stars

He counts the stars and calls them all by name.

—Psalms 147:4 NLT

I knew what I wanted to be a writer when I was five years old. So, I went to work, learned my A, B, Cs and how to make cursive letters with a pencil. Then I learned how to assemble a sentence and eventually an entire story.

Sounds easy, doesn't it?

Don't tell my secret, but I'm still learning how to write 80 years later, and I'm still reaching for the stars. In other words, I haven't arrived, yet, and that's part of the fun.

Meanwhile, I set goals every day. Those goals sometimes are long-term like finishing first grade without flunking out of recess or learning how to play the C scale on the piano—with both hands.

Maybe you want to earn enough money to buy a bicycle. That takes some planning, work and patience. Maybe you want to give a valentine to the pretty little girl that sits across from you in second grade. Only you're too bashful to talk to her during recess. (No wonder you flunked out of recess.)

Here are some suggestions about setting goals, reaching for the stars.

First, don't count the cost. You won't know the cost until you reach your goal.

For example: It cost me a nickel to buy a pencil when I was a boy. It's cost me a lifetime to become a writer.

Second, plan. You probably already know how to coax your mother into giving you a cookie for a snack. Big folks call that strategizing. In other words, how do you expect to get something done. For example, if you plan to become a professional person like a doctor, lawyer, preacher or teacher, you're going to spend lots of years in school. Or maybe you want to fix cars. So, you attend a technical school or learn your trade on the job. In any event, it will take time to reach your goal.

Third, sweat. That's a short word for work. Roll up your sleeves and put your brain in gear. If you don't spend time and effort to reach your star, you'll flame out.

Fourth, don't whimper. You're going to run into hard times—many times—while you're accomplishing your goal, depending on whether you want a cookie or a high school diploma.

Fifth, make the journey an adventure. Too many people define adventure as risky and dangerous and fail to realize that it can be an exciting and remarkable experience.

My parents encouraged me to pick a star to follow. They didn't pressure me to become a doctor, a lawyer, a teacher or a preacher. They said: "Be anything you want to be, and do it to the best of your ability."

Well, I've already told you about the star that I picked. It's been a great adventure, and one I would choose again. Keep in mind, however, that I haven't reached my star. I'm still learning how to write.

Playing to Win

I have fought the good fight. I have finished the race. I have kept the faith.

—2 Timothy 4:7 NIV

Most of us like to win.

When I play tag, I don't want to be "it." I want to dodge, run and to keep you from touching me.

When I play computer games, I want to score the most points, to knock off as many of the bad guys as I can—to win.

I also want to bring home a report card with all A grades. I want to win the perfect attendance pin, to be picked for the best part in a play and to be the pitcher on the team.

In other words, I want to feel important, to feel good, to earn the applause of my classmates, my parents and my brothers and sisters even though they probably will be jealous and will make fun of me.

Your great-grandad likes to win. He's been winning for years and years. However, he learned that winning ain't all it's cracked up to be.

Let me give you an example:

Your great-grandad ran in track while in college were he learned that "if you run in circles long enough, you will be known as a wheel." (That's a joke in case you missed it.) And I secretly wanted to be known as a wheel, an important person, a popular guy, a big-shot.

Know what? I learned that several other guys were faster than I was on the track, and I began losing races. Talk about a "downer." I kept smiling, but inside I was crying. You see, I wasn't used to losing.

I learned an important lesson, however. I call it "true grit," which means that you keep trying to do your best even though you may not win a race, a ball game or get the lead role in a play or earn the best grades.

It's the effort, the trying, that counts.

Now, I know you are going to argue about not wanting to practice the piano or to spend hours and hours learning how to catch or to hit a ball. In my case, I didn't want to play the piano, but I wanted to play ball. I could never play the piano well, but I could catch and hit a ball.

The reason I'm offering this advice is that anything worth doing is worth doing well even though you don't win or even though nobody notices, applauds or hands you an award.

Be careful, too, about the teams you select in your life. For example, I like a professional baseball team, and I want that team to win. It's okay if I cheer and get excited about my favorite team. Keep in mind, however, that I am not a member of the team, and I am not responsible for the team winning or losing.

So, don't feel as though you are a winner if your team wins the World Series, or that you should hang your head and cry if your team loses. You have your own games to win and to lose.

The good news is that you can be a member of a team with a perfect record. The coach has a special place for you to play during this lifetime—and the next. All you have to do is to join the team. You'll like the coach. He knows you're a winner.

Living an Adventure

You make known to me the path of life; you will fill me with joy in your presence, with eternal pleasures at your right hand.

—Psalms 16:11 NIV

Adventure is defined as a bold, risky undertaking. In other words, you're not sure whether the goblins will get you when you want a glass of milk and have to walk down a dark hallway to the kitchen. But you're brave, and you really want to get a glass of milk out of the refrig and maybe a chocolate cookie. That's being adventuresome.

Scary? Yeah, but oh what a delicious snack.

A lot of things you do in life will be scary. If you are adventuresome, you'll laugh and chase the goblins away. If you're a wimp, you'll stay in your room and play it safe.

I figure that you can take risks three ways: (1) with your body, (2) with your mind and (3) with your spirit.

When I was a kid, I once tried to eat left-handed. I had trouble getting the food off the plate and into my mouth because I am right-handed. My folks thought I was showing off, and my brother made fun of me, but I figured this was quite an adventure.

Later, I decided to be an actor in a third-grade play. I worried, however, that I might forget my lines, but I practiced and practiced. Guess what? I liked being on stage so much that I volunteered to be in more plays all through grade school, high school and college. I could have been a movie star, but I had other things to do.

I also began traveling to new places on my bicycle, and later I traveled to several foreign countries in airplanes. Your great-grandma and I spent more than 50 years exploring the back roads of Oregon in our car. We learned something new during every adventure.

Most of us won't admit it, but we often are too lazy or too scared to learn new things. Did you know that memorizing how to spell a new word and learning its meaning is an adventure?

It's often a lot easier to play computer games than it is to work on your algebra assignment. It's okay to play computer games. Take my advice, however, and fill your mind with new things every day of your life.

Writing this book has been an adventure. I knew it would take a lot of time and a lot of thinking as I wrote down all of these words. I knew that I might not finish the book or that my great-grandchildren might never read it. Yet, writing the book has been what I call an adventure.

You will take another adventure during your life. It's what grownups refer to as a spiritual adventure. In other words, deciding what god to walk with during this lifetime and the next.

You know how your great-grandad feels about this spiritual adventure, but it's a decision that you must make for yourself.

So, my advice is to check it out.

And don't let the goblins keep you from walking down a dark hallway to get a glass of milk.

Make each step of your life an adventure.

Touching All Your Bases

Do your best to present yourself to God as one approved, a worker who does not need to be ashamed and who correctly handles the word of truth.

—2 Timothy 2:15 NIV

In case you have forgotten, my kids are your grandparents. If you believe they are old, you know that I'm ancient.

In any event, your grandparents were athletes. One was a track star. Three of them played baseball, and I often reminded them to "touch all your bases" before a game. As you probably know, if you hit a home run and fail to touch a base, you could be called "out."

So, my advice to you is to "touch all your bases" if you want to live an exciting and rewarding life.

Here's how I view it:

First off, you need to take care of your health. When I was in high school, I realized for the first time that my grandparents were "really old" and that I might live a hundred years.

So, I decided to protect my health by not drinking liquor, by not smoking cigarettes and by not doing drugs.

If you want to remain trim and slim, you need to lay off things like potato chips and bacon and eat a lot of green stuff. And don't eat a second portion at a meal. You also need to exercise. Okay, so you're running around 18 hours a day while you're young. Keep it up for the next hundred years. And lay off booze, beer, drugs and cigarettes. Don't experiment. Just follow your great-grandad's advice and thank him about 50 years from now.

It's also important to choose work you want to do because you will be doing a lot of it for a long time. Don't be a doctor, a lawyer or a writer unless you want to do that kind of work. Fortunately, girls can now have a career outside the home, something that was hard for girls to do back in the days while I was growing up.

If you decide to get hitched, don't base your selection on the love bug that bites you. Check out the other person. Hire a detective to find out something about the person's family history. Make certain that both of you believe in the same things. Otherwise, you will be what the good book calls "unevenly yoked." If you ever attempt to drive a team of horses who refuse to travel in the same direction, you get my point.

Finally, selecting a god to follow is the most important base you will ever touch. If you are a kid, you probably will follow what your parents believe about the hereafter and how to get there. One of these days, however, you will be on your own, probably in college, and will be free to search for answers to questions every person asks: Who am I, and why am I here?

You know my thoughts on this subject. I picked Jesus to follow. As a result I know who I am, why I'm here and how I should touch all my bases.

About the Author

Dean Rea is a former newspaper journalist and a retired university professor who lives in Eugene, Oregon.

He was born and reared on a farm and began his newspaper career while a student at Southwest Missouri State (now Missouri State University) in Springfield. In 1951 he received a graduate degree in journalism from the University of Missouri.

He edited an armed services newspaper during his Air Force career and later worked as an editor, reporter and photographer for a dozen weekly and daily newspapers in the Midwest and in Oregon, including *The Hood River News, The Bulletin* in Bend and *The Register-Guard* in Eugene.

He also taught journalism at the University of Montana, at Biola University in Los Angeles County and at the University of Oregon, ending in 2008.

Dean and his wife Lou have spent their vacations for more than a half-century exploring the back roads of Oregon.